LULLABIES

Around The World

Featuring Designs From The Hallmark Collection

Piano • Vocal

LULLABIES
Around The World

Featuring Designs
From The Hallmark Collection

SWEET DREAMS AND GLAD AWAKENINGS BE THINE!

HAL•LEONARD
CORPORATION

7777 W. BLUEMOUND RD. P.O. BOX 13819 MILWAUKEE, WI 53213

Arranged by Bill Boyd

ISBN 0-7935-3525-5 (Softcover)
ISBN 0-7935-3777-0 (Hardcover)

Published by HAL LEONARD CORPORATION
P.O. Box 13819, 7777 West Bluemound Road
Milwaukee, WI 53213 USA

Contents

Introduction

What tradition is as old, or as universal, or as precious, as that of the singing of lullabies? Surely wherever and for as long as families have existed, parents have sung their children to sleep.

As ancient as this tradition is, however, it is not outdated. Indeed, today, when the winds of social change blow faster and harder than ever before, the sanctuary of the lullaby is more necessary than ever. When the forces of an increasingly mobile society have severed people from their past—when the pace of life has increased to a frantic rush—when upheavals within and without the family have taken an unprecedented toll—now, especially now, is the comfort of a lullaby a treasure beyond price.

What is a lullaby? A textbook answer, though far from completely satisfactory, might at least shed some light on the subject. The word "lullaby" itself comes from two roots buried deep in the history of the English language. "Lulla" means "to soothe," and it is still used today in the verb "to lull." It may have had its origin in onomatopoeia: it is easy to imagine a parent improvising a melody for a sleepy child, with no more words than "la-la, la-la."

"By," or "bye," is an old word meaning "sleep." When a mother sings "Bye baby bunting" (see page 22), she's telling the child to sleep. She is *not* telling the infant "goodbye" in any sense. (The latter word originated as a contraction of "God be with ye" and is totally irrelevant here.) So "lullaby" means to soothe a child to sleep.

In other languages, the terminology is sometimes imitative (the Spanish "nana" and Italian "ninnananna"), but just as often descriptive: the French "berceuse" means "rocker"; the German "Wiegenlied" and Spanish "canción de cuna" mean "cradle song."

So much for the scholarly approach. The real meaning of a lullaby is something vastly deeper than a dictionary definition. A lullaby is not a thing; it is a place— a separate world, inhabited by the parent and child alone. It is a place where time stands still, where the distractions of the day no longer exist. It is a bond between the one who cares and the one cared for; a closeness, a tenderness beyond the reach of more mundane activities.

A lullaby is a place of magic and enchantment—of monsters vanquished, castles secured, peace attained. It may be a place of stories, of doing, or merely of being. It is a place where two hearts beat so closely that they quiet one another.

This book is a window to that enchanted world—a world that encompasses all of this globe we call Earth. There are lullabies here from far-flung places and times, and yet for all their differences of language, tune, or imagery, they have more in common than not.

Over 25 traditional lullabies are presented here, in arrangements specially written to be easy to play or sing. Each is accompanied by a brief note illuminating the background or meaning of the song, and each is complemented by designs from the Hallmark Collection. It is our hope that this book serves as a stepping-stone for you and your children, for many journeys into the happy and peaceful land of lullaby.

Abiyoyo

The word "abiyoyo" has no translatable meaning; it is merely a collection of nonsense syllables. The song, which comes from Cape Province, South Africa, concludes a bedtime story about a monster. The youngster is told that he or she can overcome the terrible beast by chanting these hypnotic words. In a sense, the incantation really works—but it is the child that is subdued.

Abiyoyo

South African

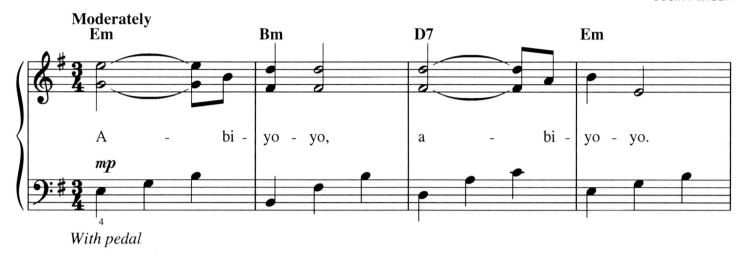

A - bi - yo - yo, a - bi - yo - yo.

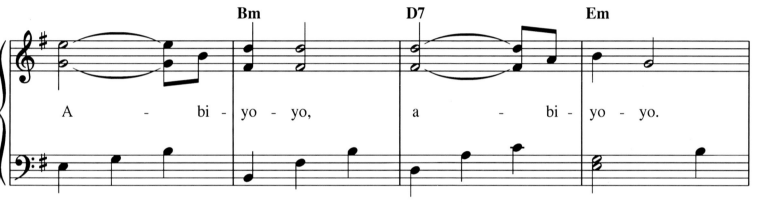

A - bi - yo - yo, a - bi - yo - yo.

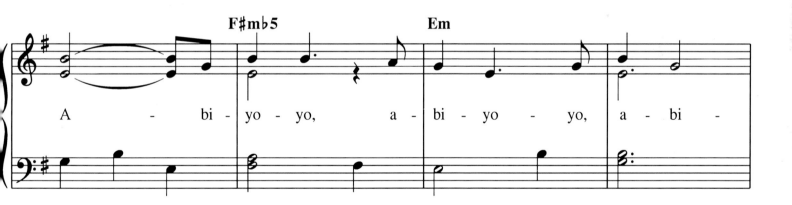

A - bi - yo - yo, a - bi - yo - yo, a - bi -

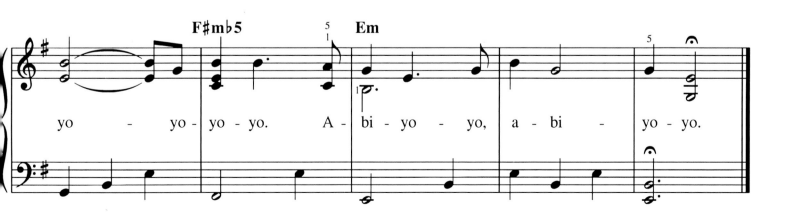

yo - yo - yo - yo. A - bi - yo - yo, a - bi - yo - yo.

All The Pretty Little Horses

This beloved folk song from the American South employs a device used in lullabies the world over: the "catalog" of presents—in this case, horses. The purpose is not so much to bribe the child into going to sleep (after all, will all these animals really show up at the door in the morning?) as to set the stage for pleasant dreams.

All The Pretty Little Horses

American

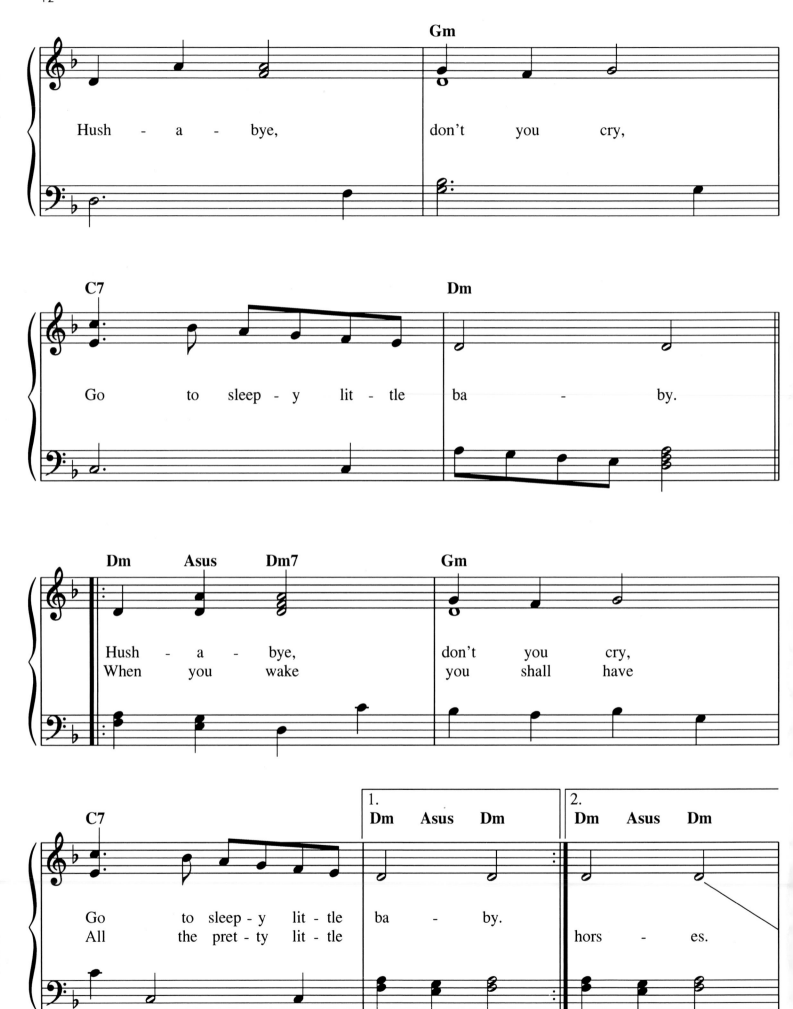

All Through The Night

This Welsh folk tune was first published in 1784, with the title "Ar Hyd Y Nos." The English words given here were written a century later, by Sir Harold Boulton (1859–1935). Boulton refers to Christmas in his second and third verses—a theme not found in the original Welsh lyrics. Although this association has stuck, it seems a shame to restrict this beautiful lullaby to a single season of the year; the first verse can be sung at any time.

All Through The Night

Welsh

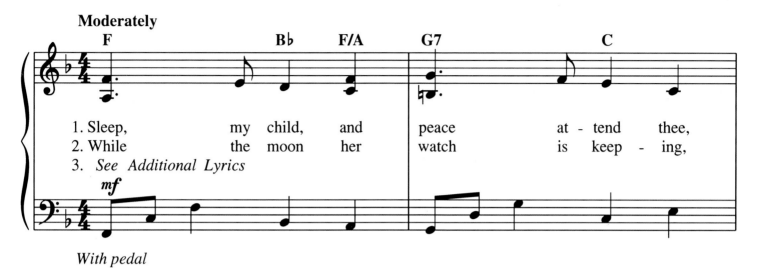

1. Sleep,   my child,   and   peace   at - tend   thee,
2. While   the moon   her   watch   is   keep -   ing,
3. *See Additional Lyrics*

With pedal

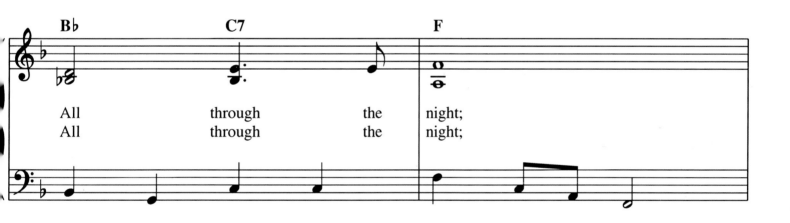

All   through   the   night;
All   through   the   night;

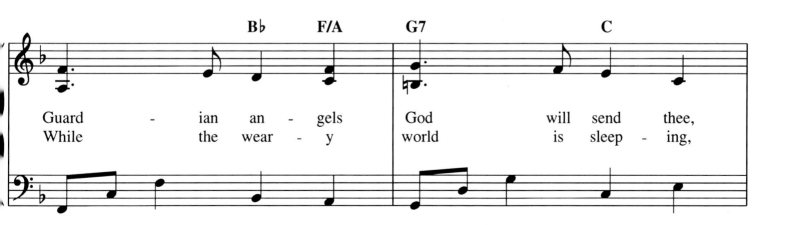

Guard   -   ian an   -   gels   God   will send   thee,
While   the wear - y   world   is sleep - ing,

All through the night.
All through the night.

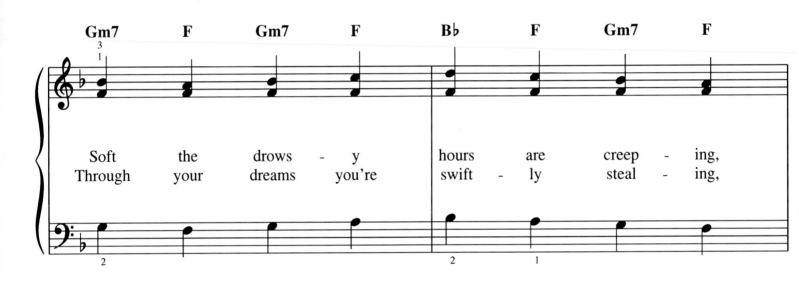

Soft the drows - y hours are creep - ing,
Through your dreams you're swift - ly steal - ing,

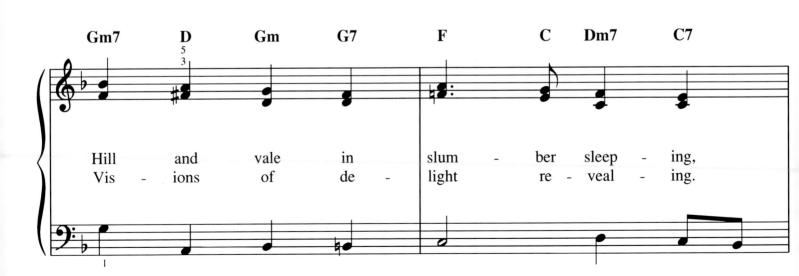

Hill and vale in slum - ber sleep - ing,
Vis - ions of de - light re - veal - ing.

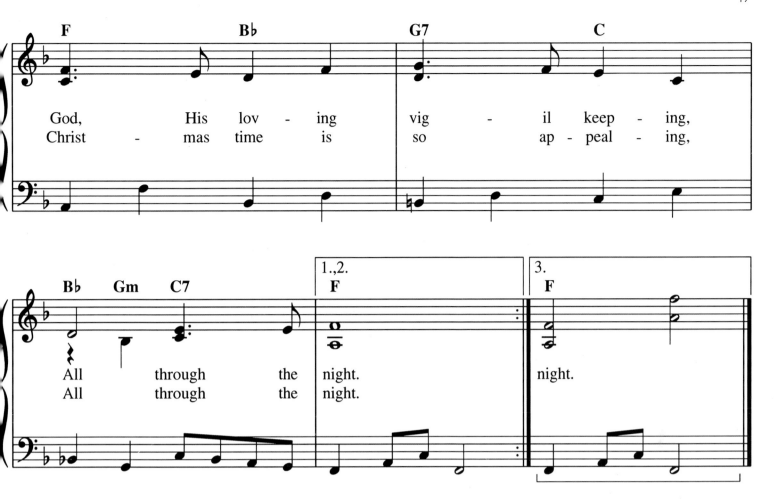

God,   His   lov - ing   vig -   il   keep - ing,
Christ - mas time   is   so   ap - peal - ing,

All   through   the   night.
All   through   the   night.   night.

Additional Lyrics

3. You, my God, a Babe of wonder,
    All through the night;
    Dreams you dream can't break from thunder,
    All through the night.
    Children's dreams cannot be broken;
    Life is but a lovely token.
    Christmas should be softly spoken
    All through the night.

Brahms' Lullaby

Johannes Brahms (1833–1897) composed the melody for this, perhaps the most famous lullaby in the world, in 1868; he based the original piano accompaniment on an Austrian *Ländler*, a waltzlike folk song. Natalia MacFarren's faithful English translation of the anonymous German words has succeeded in keeping the word "bedight" in our dictionaries, if not in our everyday vocabularies.

Brahms' Lullaby

German

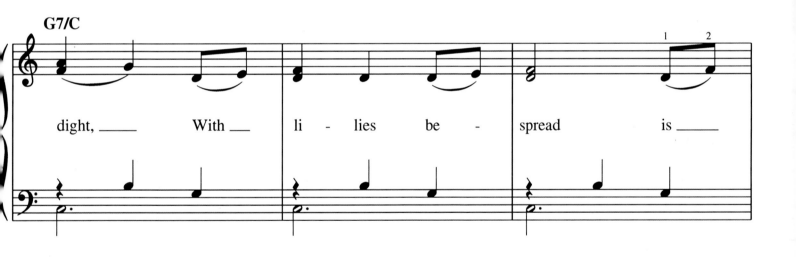

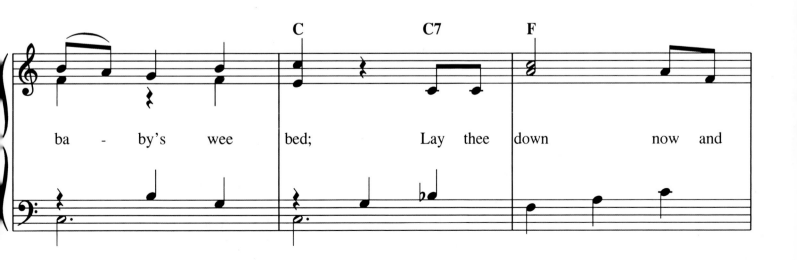

© Hallmark Licensing, Inc.

Bye Baby Bunting

The word "bunting" is a term of endearment, but with at least two possible derivations. On one hand, it may refer to a small bird (compare "Can Ye Sew Cushions," where the mother calls the baby "birdie"). On the other, it might derive from "bundle," with the twin connotations of the baby being "a bundle of joy" and the necessity of wrapping the child (as expressed at the end of the lyrics) to keep it warm and comfortable.

British

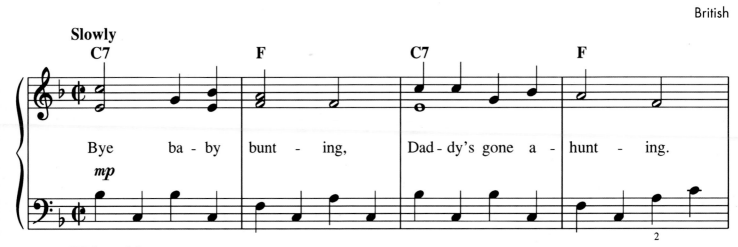

With pedal

From the Hallmark Historical Collection. The original postcard by Ellen H. Clapsaddle
was published around 1900 by International Art Publishing Company.

— ◆ —

Can Ye Sew Cushions

Scottish lullabies, perhaps reflecting the severity of the
countryside, tend to be bleaker than most. (See also
"Oh, Hush Thee, My Baby.") In a cottage during a
storm, a mother rocks her crying baby. Her thoughts
alternate between calming the child and expressing her
own fears—for her husband, who is at sea in the gale,
and for her children, who suffer want. "Black's the life
that I lead wi' ye" is an expression of despair, but not
of blame; it's clear when the mother calls the baby "my
bonnie wee lamb" that she loves her children dearly.

Can Ye Sew Cushions

Scottish

hie   and baw   bird - ie, My   bon - nie wee   lamb.

Faster

Refrain C   G/C   C

Hee - o - wee - o,   What will I do wi' ye?   Black's the life that

G/C   C   G/C   C

I   lead wi' ye.   Ma - ny o' ye,   lit - tle for to gi' ye,

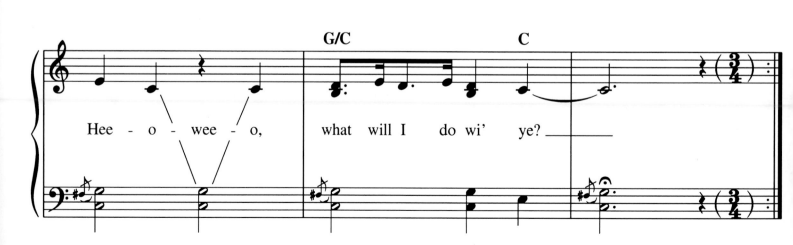

G/C   C

Hee - o - wee - o,   what will I do wi' ye?

Additional Lyrics

2. I biggit* the cradle all on the tree top
   And the wind it did blaw, and the cradle did rock.
   And hie and baw birdie, And hie and baw lamb,
   And hie and baw birdie, My bonnie wee lamb.
   Refrain

3. Now hush-a-ba, lammie, and hush-a-ba, dear,
   Now hush-a-ba, lammie, thy minnie+ is here.
   And hie and baw birdie, And hie and baw lamb,
   And hie and baw birdie, My bonnie wee lamb.
   Refrain

4. The wild wind is ravin', thy minnie's heart's sair;
   The wild wind is ravin', and you dinna care.
   And hie and baw birdie, And hie and baw lamb,
   And hie and baw birdie, My bonnie wee lamb.
   Refrain

5. Sing ba-la-loo, lammie, sing ba-la-loo, dear,
   Does the wee lammie ken that his daddie's no' here?
   And hie and baw birdie, And hie and baw lamb,
   And hie and baw birdie, My bonnie wee lamb.
   Refrain

6. Ye're rockin' fu' sweetly upon my warm knee,
   But your daddie's a-rockin' upon the salt sea.
   And hie and baw birdie, And hie and baw lamb,
   And hie and baw birdie, My bonnie wee lamb.
   Refrain

biggit: built
+*minnie: mother*

© Hallmark Licensing, Inc.

Chinese Baby-Song

By definition, lullabies are sung to put children to sleep. But here is a song designed to wake them up. The imagery of a snail peeking out of its shell is a humorous but apt picture of the baby, perhaps playfully hiding from its parents, emerging from under the covers.

Chinese Baby-Song

Chinese

Repeat ad infinitum

OF ALL DEAR ANNIVERSARIES THY BIRTHDAY IS THE DEAREST.

From the Hallmark Historical Collection. This card was originally printed in the 1880s.

Cotton-Eyed Joe

Who was this Cotton-Eyed Joe? Probably not a real person. In any case, don't expect to discover much about him in the song, which doesn't actually tell a story, but rather uses the character as the basis for a series of disconnected, freely invented episodes—think of him as a Southern relative of "Old Dan Tucker." This won't put the little ones to sleep, but it will give them plenty of bedtime entertainment.

Cotton-Eyed Joe

American

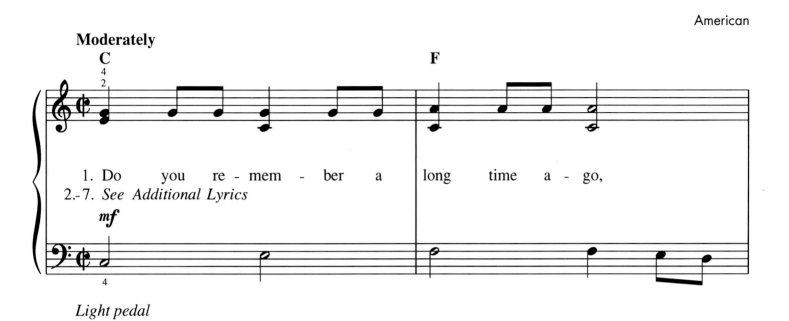

1. Do you re-mem-ber a long time a-go,
2.-7. *See Additional Lyrics*

Light pedal

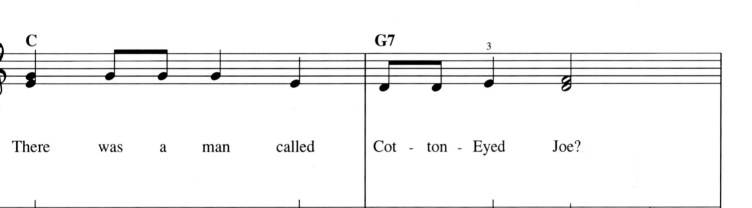

There was a man called Cot-ton-Eyed Joe?

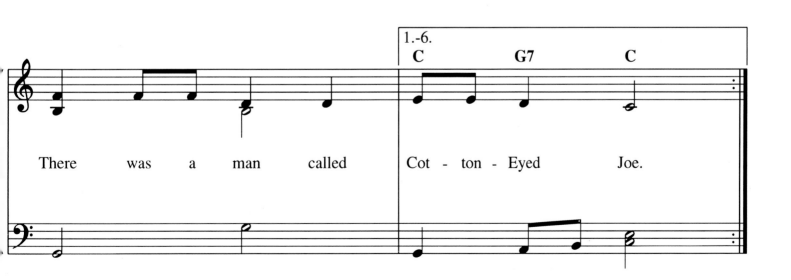

There was a man called Cot-ton-Eyed Joe.

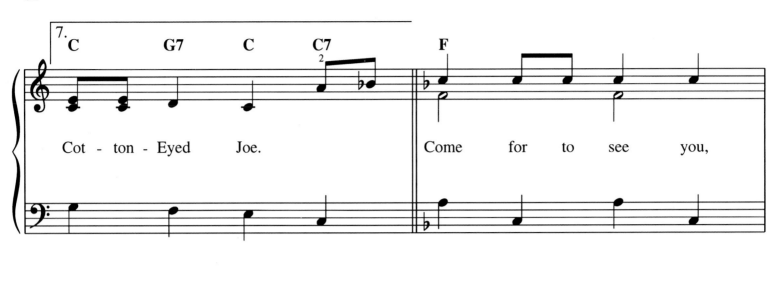

7.

C   **G7**   **C**   **C7**   **F**

Cot - ton - Eyed Joe.   Come for to see you,

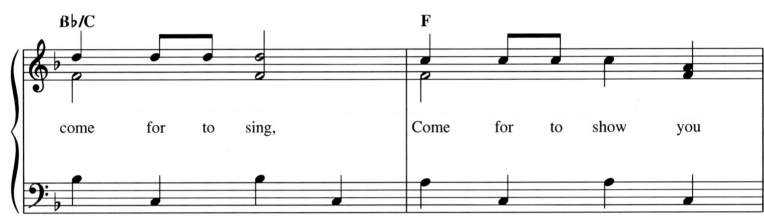

Bb/C   **F**

come for to sing,   Come for to show you

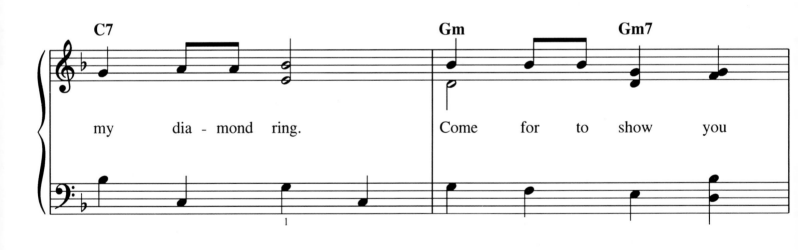

C7   **Gm**   **Gm7**

my dia - mond ring.   Come for to show you

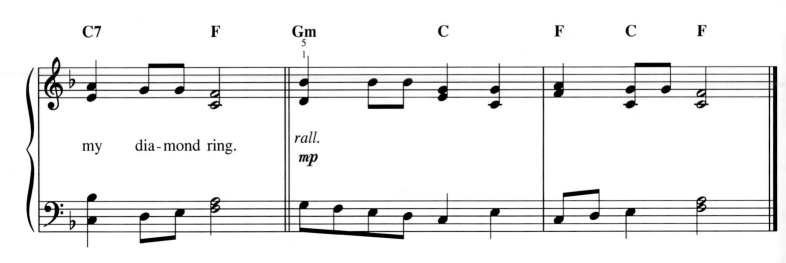

C7   **F**   **Gm**   **C**   **F**   **C**   **F**

my dia-mond ring.   *rall.*
         mp

Additional Lyrics

2. I could have been married a long time ago,
   If it hadn't a-been for Cotton-Eyed Joe...

3. Old bull fiddle and a shoe-string bow,
   Wouldn't play nothin' but Cotton-Eyed Joe...

4. Play it fast or play it slow,
   Didn't play nothin' but Cotton-Eyed Joe...

5. Don't you remember a long time ago,
   Daddy worked a man called Cotton-Eyed Joe...

6. Where do you come from? Where do you go?
   Where do you come from Cotton-Eyed Joe?...

7. Come for to see you, come for to sing,
   Come for to show you my diamond ring...

© Hallmark Licensing, Inc.

Cradle Hymn

Isaac Watts (1674–1748), "Father of the English Hymn," penned the words to this song, which contrast the comfort of the present child with the sufferings of Christ. French philosopher, writer, and musician Jean Jacques Rousseau (1712–1778) wrote the tune used here, which is often mistaken for the American folk song "Go Tell Aunt Rhody." As is often the case with hymns, the words have been set to other music as well.

Cradle Hymn

French

1. Hush, my _____ babe, lie still and slum - ber,
2.,3. *See Additional Lyrics*

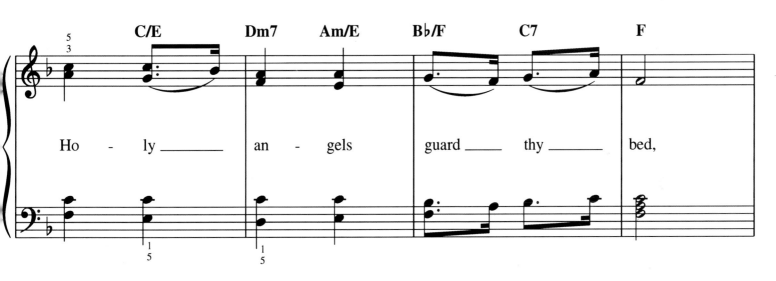

Ho - ly _____ an - gels guard _____ thy _____ bed,

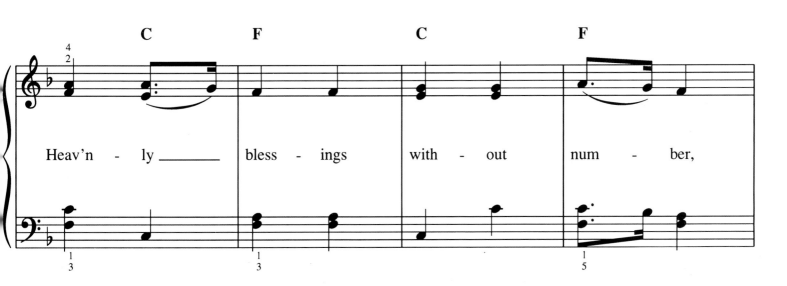

Heav'n - ly _____ bless - ings with - out num - ber,

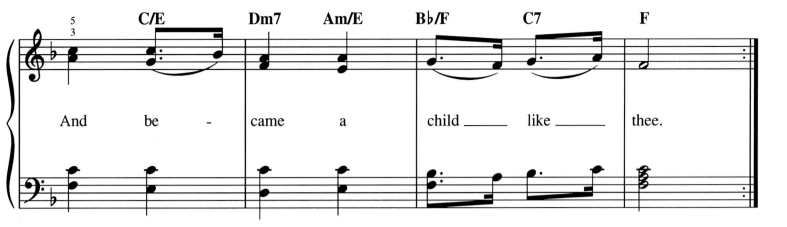

And be - came a child ____ like ____ thee.

Additional Lyrics

2. Soft and easy is thy cradle,
   Coarse and hard thy Savior lay,
   When His birthplace was a stable,
   And His softest bed was hay.
   Oh, to tell the wonderous story,
   How His foes abused their King;
   How they killed the Lord of glory,
   Makes me angry when I sing.

3. Hush, my child, I did not chide thee,
   Though my song may seem so hard,
   'Tis thy mother sits beside thee,
   And her arms shall be thy guard.
   May'st thou learn to know and fear Him,
   Love and serve Him all thy days;
   Then to dwell forever near Him,
   Tell His love and sing His praise.

© Hallmark Licensing, Inc.

Cradle Song

Most lullabies (in Western countries, at least) are set in major keys, which helps to make them bright and cheerful. In contrast, this traditional Swedish lullaby is set in a minor key, which gives it a contemplative mood. The brief excursions to G major are like shafts of light from the setting sun as twilight closes gently in. This song was made popular outside its native country by soprano Jenny Lind (1820–1887), who was known as "the Swedish Nightingale."

Cradle Song

Swedish

© Hallmark Licensing, Inc.

Duermete Niño Lindo

(Sleep, Pretty Baby)

In countries influenced by Christianity, it is only natural that some of the lullabies would draw upon the image of the infant Jesus, as this one does. (See also "All Through The Night" and "Cradle Hymn."). In fact, the words of this song are written as if they are sung by the Virgin Mary. The word "alarru" comes from the verb "arrullar," which means "to lull."

Duermete Niño Lindo
(Sleep, Pretty Baby)

Latin American

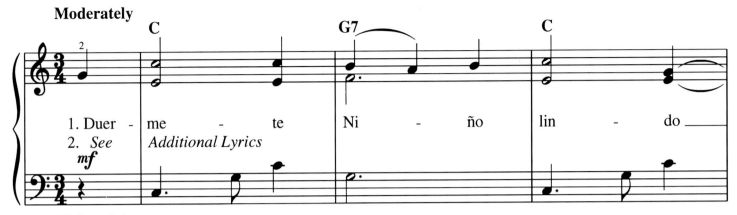

Moderately

1. Duer - me - te Ni - ño lin - do ___
2. *See* *Additional Lyrics*

With pedal

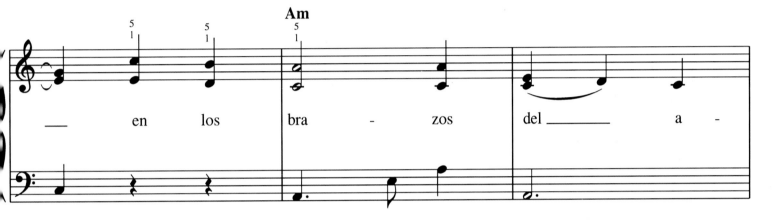

___ en los bra - zos del ___ a -

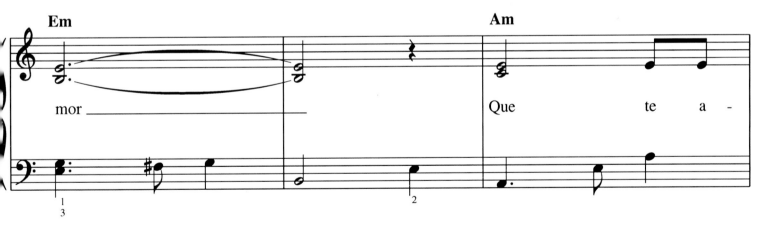

mor ___ Que te a -

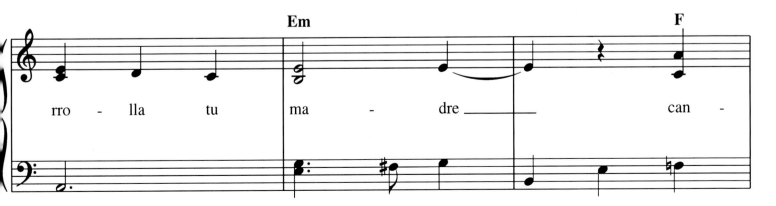

rro - lla tu ma - dre ___ can -

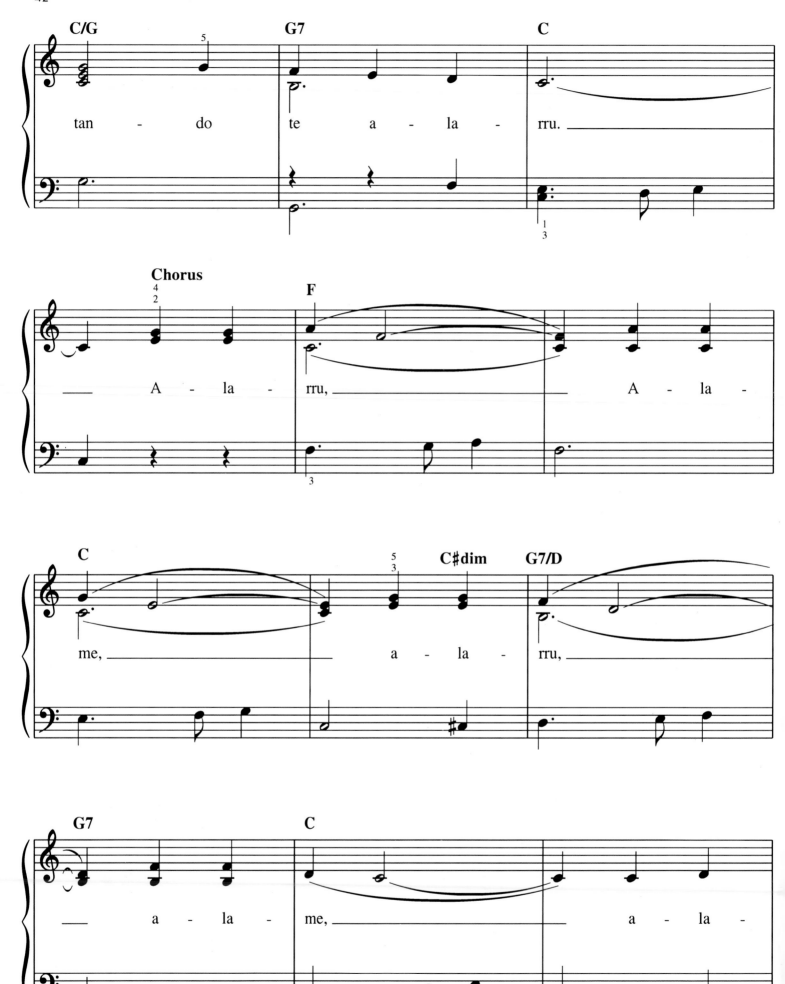

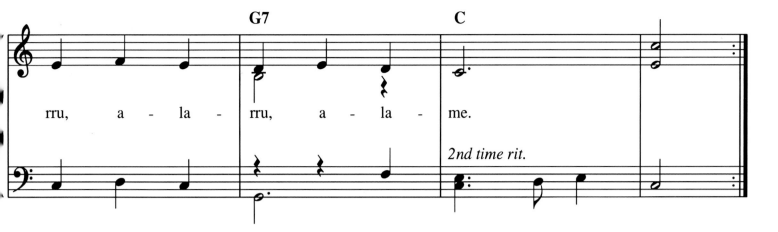

G7 **C**

rru,   a - la - | rru,   a - la - | me.

2nd time rit.

Additional Lyrics

2. No temas a Herodes
   que nada te has de hacer
   Que en los brazos de tu madre
   Nadie te ha de ofender.
   Chorus

Translation

1. O hush my pretty baby,
   Sleeping in the arms of love,
   While your mother sings you
   A lullaby from above.
   Alarru, alame,...

2. Have no fear of Herod
   He can do no harm to you;
   Rest in the arms of your mother,
   While she sings alarru.
   Alarru, alame,...

© Hallmark Licensing, Inc.

Golden Slumbers

This favorite British lullaby goes back at least as far as the seventeenth century. The words were given a twist when the Beatles used them, with a new tune, on their album *Abbey Road*—pairing the song with "Carry That Weight" for a thoroughly ironic effect. It is fervently hoped that there is still a place for the gentle spirit of the original.

Golden Slumbers

British

Slowly

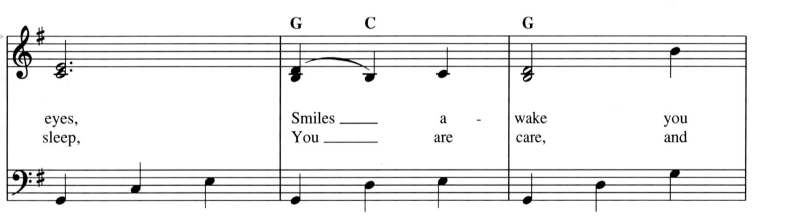

Gold - en slum - bers kiss your
Care _____ is heav - y, there - fore

mp

With pedal

eyes,   Smiles _____ a - wake you
sleep,   You _____ are care, and

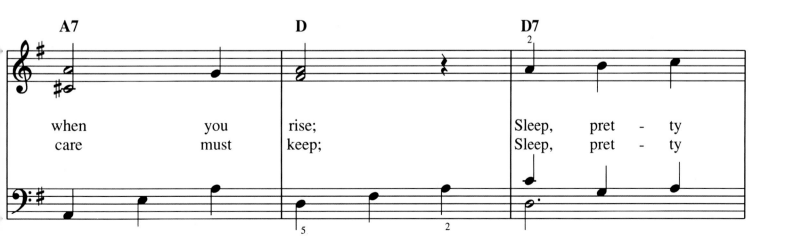

when   you   rise;   Sleep, pret - ty
care   must   keep;   Sleep, pret - ty

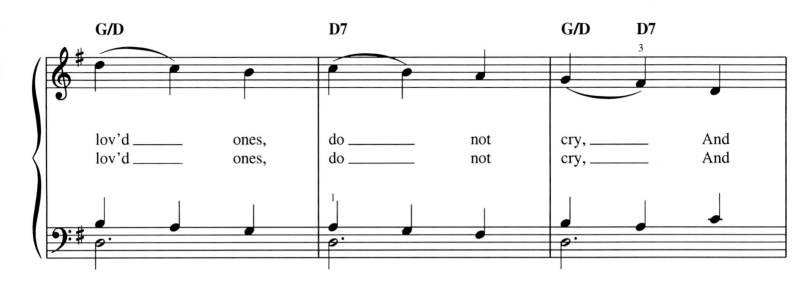

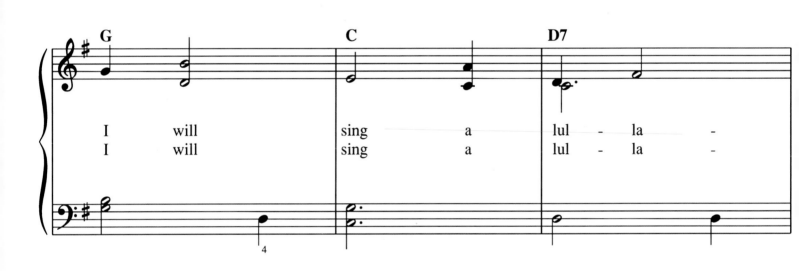

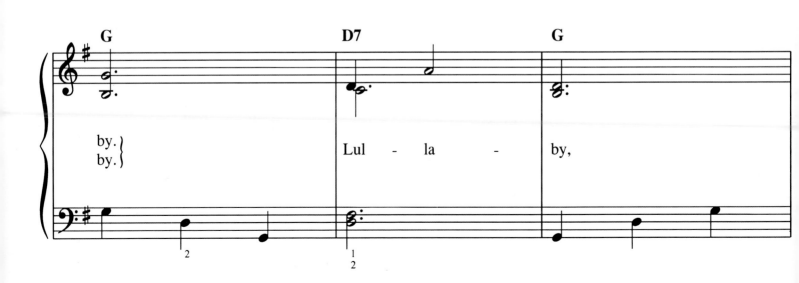

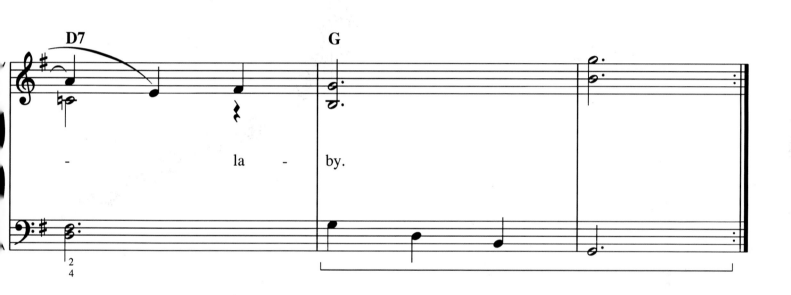

Hush, Little Baby

In its present form, this lullaby comes from the Southern Appalachians, though some scholars trace its roots back to England. It surely is one of the most popular lullabies with American children, for a variety of reasons: the engaging melodic repetition, the clever rhymes ("dog named Rover"), the variety of "presents," and the reassurance that, no matter what happens, they are still loved.

Hush, Little Baby

American

Hush, lit - tle ba - by, don't say a word;
if that bil - ly goat won't pull,

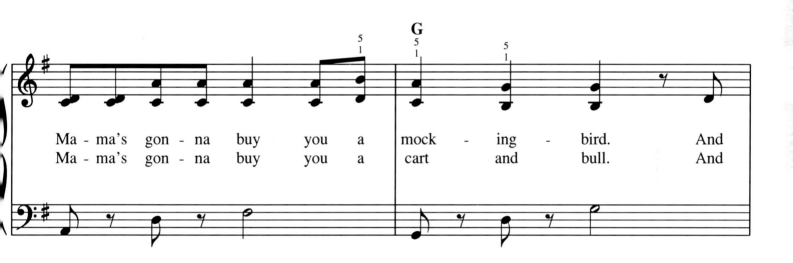

Ma - ma's gon - na buy you a mock - ing - bird. And
Ma - ma's gon - na buy you a cart and bull. And

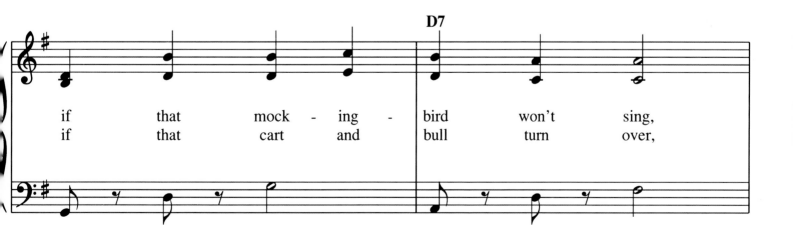

if that mock - ing - bird won't sing,
if that cart and bull turn over,

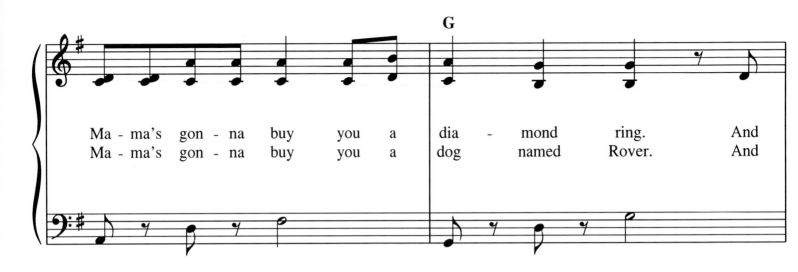

Ma - ma's gon - na buy you a dia - mond ring. And
Ma - ma's gon - na buy you a dog named Rover. And

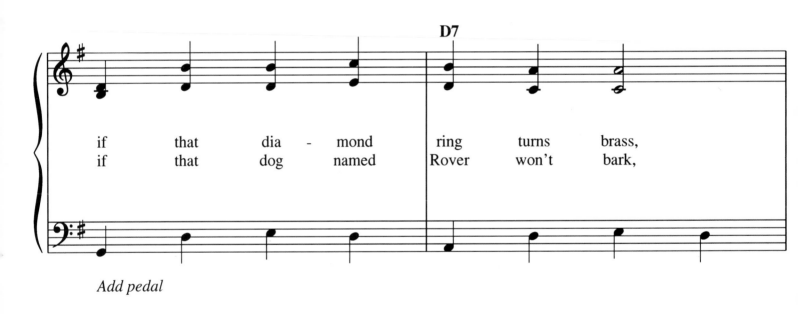

if that dia - mond ring turns brass,
if that dog named Rover won't bark,

Add pedal

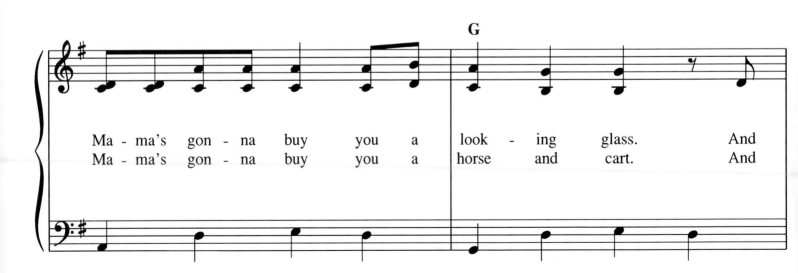

Ma - ma's gon - na buy you a look - ing glass. And
Ma - ma's gon - na buy you a horse and cart. And

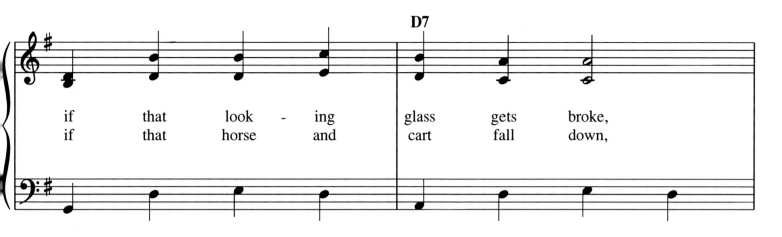

if   that   look - ing   glass   gets   broke,
if   that   horse and   cart   fall   down,

Ma - ma's gon - na buy you a   bil - ly goat.   And
You'll still be the sweetest lit - tle   ba - by in town.

SWEET DREAMS AND GLAD AWAKENINGS BE THINE!

Liebestraum
(Dream Of Love)

The Hungarian composer Franz Liszt (1811–1886) wrote this familiar melody, which was first published in 1847 as a song with the title "O Lieb" ("O Love") and German words by one F. Freiligrath. Three years later Liszt arranged it for solo piano, and it was released as the third of a set of three nocturnes entitled *Liebesträume* ("Love Dreams"). This gentle and ageless music is paired here with new words.

Liebestraum
(Dream Of Love)

Hungarian

Now The Day Is Over

The Rev. Sabine Baring-Gould (1834–1924) was a British clergyman, author, folk song collector, and hymn writer. He wrote "Now The Day Is Over" in 1864 as a children's hymn, along with "Onward, Christian Soldiers." His words here constitute not so much a lullaby as a bedtime prayer. They are based on Proverbs 3:24: "When thou liest down, thou shalt not be afraid; yea, thou shalt lie down, and thy sleep shall be sweet." The tune was written in 1868 by Sir Joseph Barnby (see "Sweet And Low").

British

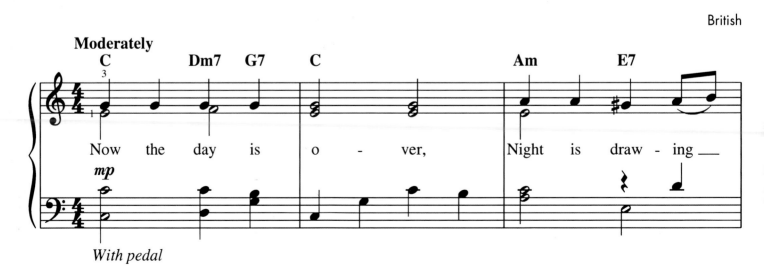

Now the day is o - ver, Night is draw - ing

Oh, Hush Thee, My Baby

Both the landscape and the history of Scotland are rocky. This bittersweet lullaby originated during one of many periods of unrest there. A verse omitted here speaks of a coming time "when sleep shall be broken by trumpet and drum," a time when, no longer a child, the youngster must concern himself with the strife that surrounds him. Till then, however, he is soothed by fantasies of a noble birth, a vast inheritance, and protection from harm.

Oh, Hush Thee, My Baby

Scottish

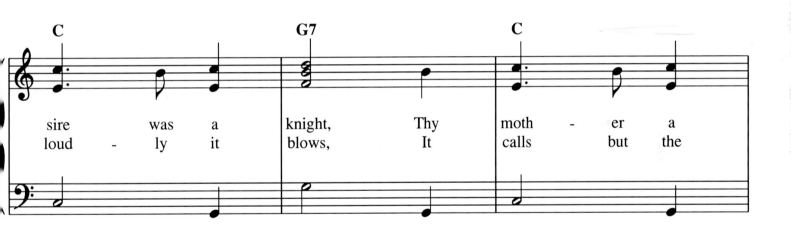

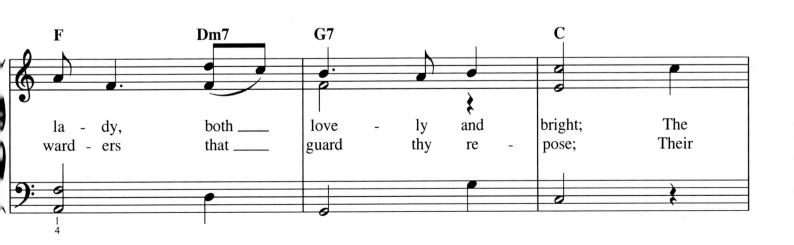

58

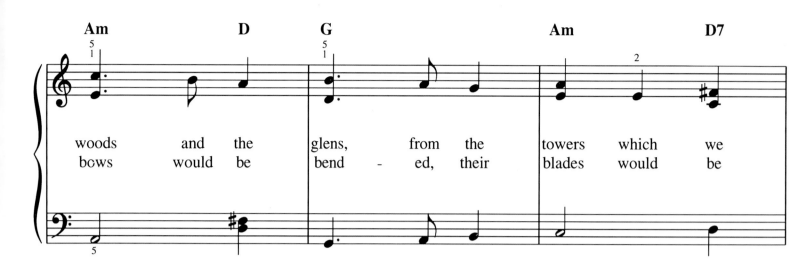

woods and the glens, from the towers which we
bows would be bended, their blades which would be

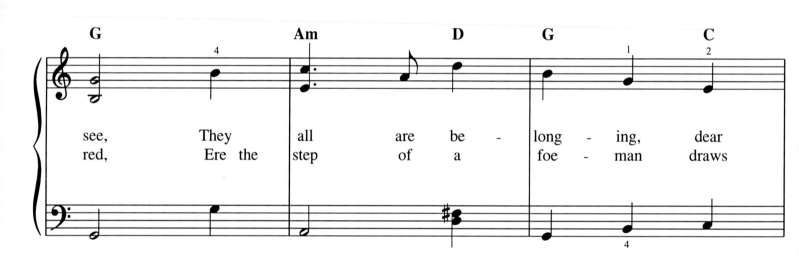

see, They all are be - long - ing, dear
red, Ere the step of a foe - man draws

ba - by, to thee.
near to thy bed.

Oh, _____ rest thee, babe,

rest thee, babe, sleep on till day! Oh,

rest thee, babe, rest thee, babe,—— sleep——— while you may!

© Hallmark Licensing, Inc.

Our Baby

This old French folk song represents the genre of "game songs," in which the words are accompanied by actions. Such songs are found all over the world, and may involve pointing, patting, tickling, or other activities; in this case, it's kissing. The following example illustrates how the song might be done: "Cheeks of rose [*kiss one cheek, then the other*], tiny toes [*kiss one foot, then the other*] has our little baby."

Our Baby

French

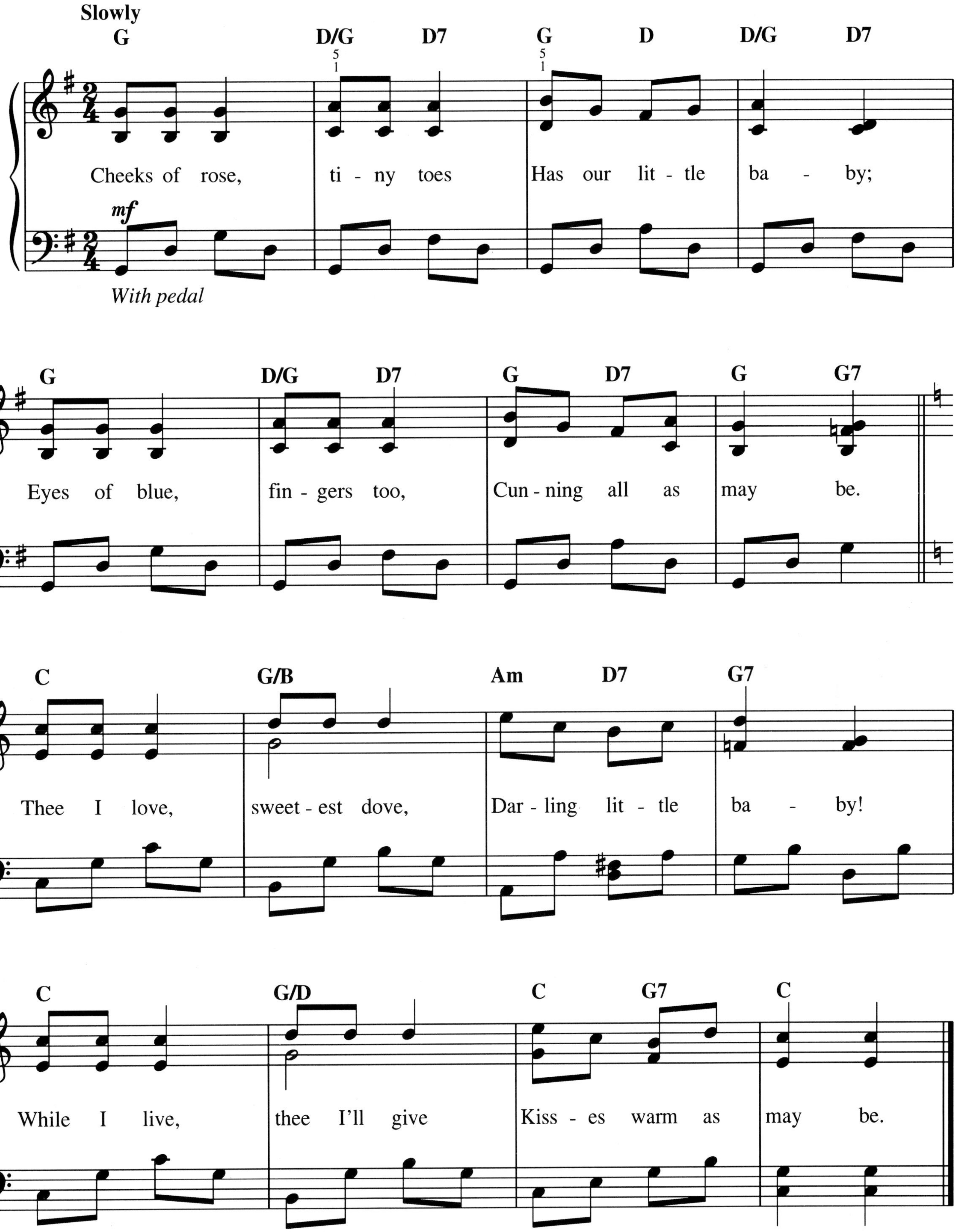

Slowly
G D/G D7 G D D/G D7
Cheeks of rose, ti - ny toes Has our lit - tle ba - by;
mf
With pedal
G D/G D7 G D7 G G7
Eyes of blue, fin - gers too, Cun - ning all as may be.
C G/B Am D7 G7
Thee I love, sweet - est dove, Dar - ling lit - tle ba - by!
C G/D C G7 C
While I live, thee I'll give Kiss - es warm as may be.

Pu'va, Pu'va, Pu'va
(Sleep, Sleep, Sleep)

In Northeastern Arizona, where the Hopi Indians live, this lullaby has been sung for untold generations. A Hopi mother sings it to the baby she bears on her back as she rocks to and fro. She sings of how, in the hot sun, the beetles, too, sometimes sleep on one another's backs. What could be a more charming picture?

Native American

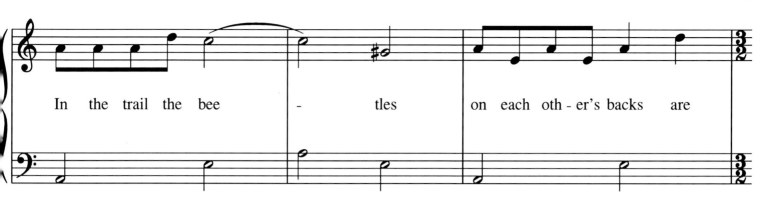

In the trail the bee - tles on each oth - er's backs are

sleep - ing. So on mine my ba - by, thou _____

sleep, _____ sleep, _____ sleep.

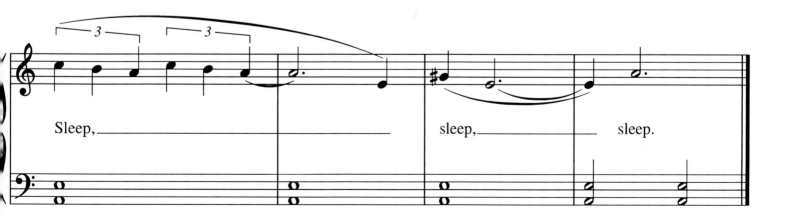

Sleep, _____ sleep, _____ sleep.

Raisins And Almonds

"Rozhinkes Mit Mandlen," as it is called in Yiddish, was written by Abraham Goldfaden (1840–1908) as part of his operetta *Shulamith*—one of 26 such stage works that earned him the title "the Father of Modern Yiddish Theatre." In this touching lullaby, which may have been based on a folk song, the mother expresses her hopes for her baby's future in figurative terms: the goat, a symbol of sustenance, represents success in business; raisins and almonds, which are sweet delicacies, represent the best that life has to offer.

Raisins And Almonds

Yiddish

At tem - ple, a wid - ow, a daugh - ter of

Zi - on, sits in a cor - ner a -

part from the throng. Her on - ly dear

ba - by she rocks close be - side her, and

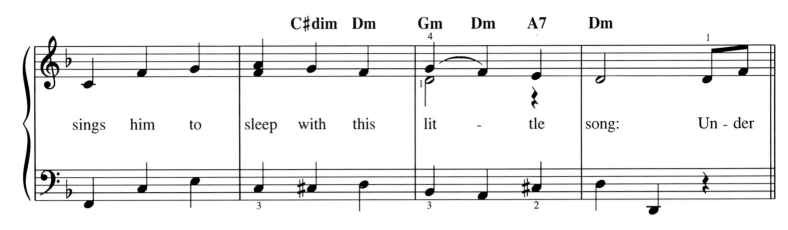

sings him to sleep with this lit - tle song: Un - der

my ba - by's cra - dle to - night stands a

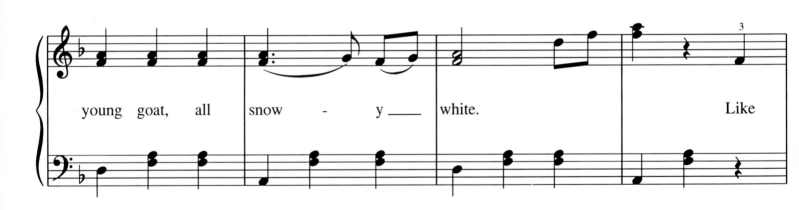

young goat, all snow - y ___ white. Like

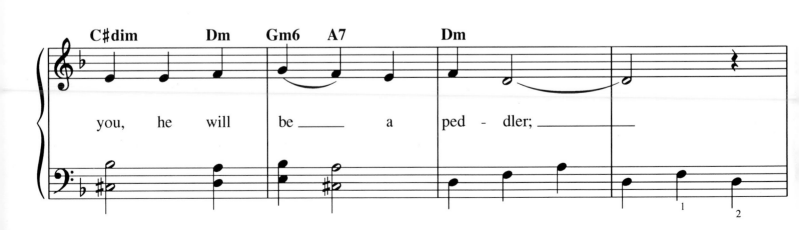

you, he will be ___ a ped - dler; ___

Rock-A-Bye, Baby

The anonymous words of this old favorite, which originally began "Hush-a-bye, baby," were first published in London around 1765. More than a century later in the United States, 15-year-old Effie Crockett (1857–1940) changed the first word and improvised a melody to sing while baby-sitting. Crockett (a relative of Davy Crockett) published the song in 1884 under the pseudonym Effie Canning. Adults concerned about the imagery of "when the bough breaks the cradle will fall" can rest assured that, in the context of the song, the descent must certainly be a gentle one.

Rock-A-Bye, Baby

American

Rock - a - bye, ba - by, on the tree top,
Hush - a - bye, ba - by, up in the sky,

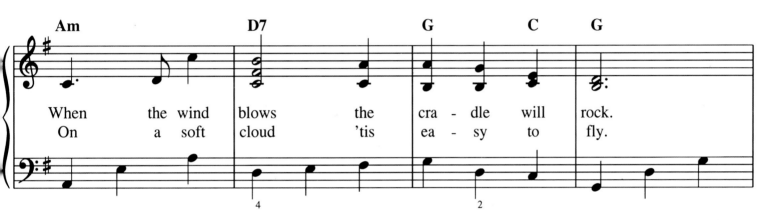

When the wind blows the cra - dle will rock.
On a soft cloud 'tis ea - sy to fly.

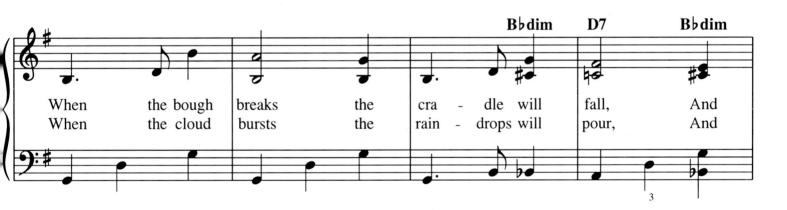

When the bough breaks the cra - dle will fall, And
When the cloud bursts the rain - drops will pour, And

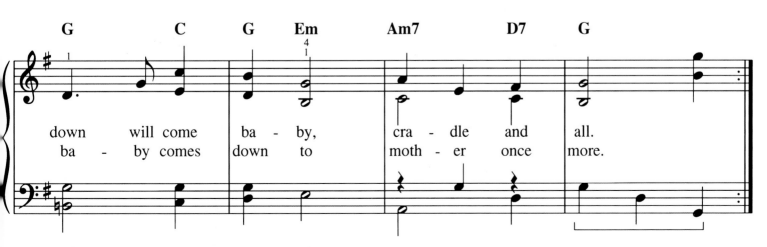

down will come ba - by, cra - dle and all.
ba - by comes down to moth - er once more.

© Hallmark Licensing, Inc.

She Will Gather Roses

This song is sung to girls among the Tsimshian Indians of British Columbia. It portrays the child as both helping with chores and enjoying the beauties of nature. The chanted "a haw haw hay hay hee" was left untranslated to help convey the flavor of the song. The many repeated notes in the bass suggest the original accompaniment of drums.

She Will Gather Roses

Native American

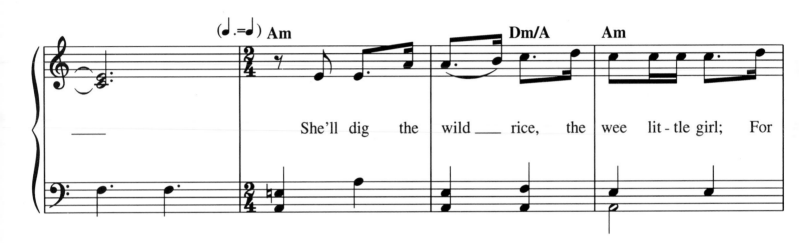

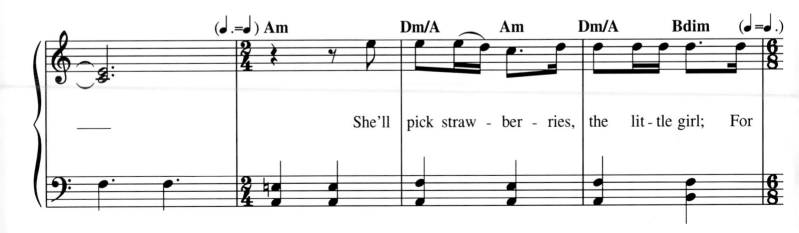

Sleep, Baby, Sleep

For hundreds of years German parents have sung their babies to sleep with "Schlaf, Kindlein, Schlaf." So popular was the lullaby that composer Richard Wagner incorporated it into his *Siegfried Idyll*, written in 1870 for his wife's birthday, in honor of their infant son Siegfried. A century earlier, the song bobbed up on the other side of the Atlantic among the Pennsylvania Dutch (originally Pennsylvania *Deutsch*, since they immigrated from Germany).

Sleep, Baby, Sleep

German

There is a place
all babies know--
it's just a yawn away--
where sleepyheads in cozy beds
can go to dream each day.
It can't be charted
by the stars,
or found upon a map,
for Dreamland lies
beyond the sighs
of wee ones as they nap.
Its fleecy clouds, like little lambs,
all frolic in the sky,
and tiny birds can sing the words to every lullaby.
Through lilac fields the rocking horses
romp without a care,
and drops of dew, in pink and blue,
are twinkling everywhere!

Sleep, Sleep, Little One, Sleep

No one knows for sure where the idea of counting sheep as a cure for insomnia originated; but one thing is certain: it is both old and widespread, as this traditional French lullaby attests. What is particularly charming here is the progression from the sheep in the pen in verse one to the "sheep" in the sky (clouds) in verse three.

Sleep, Sleep, Little One, Sleep

French

Sleep, sleep, lit-tle one, sleep.

{ There out-side are
{ Guard-ian an-gels
{ See, the sky is

all the sheep;
watch will keep;
filled with sheep;

Lambs are penned up,
There be-neath the
Like a flock the

safe from harm.
ap-ple tree
clouds drift by,

Sleep, my dar-ling,
Gath-er they sweet
Led by moon-lit

co-zy warm. }
dreams for thee. }
lul-la-by. }

Sleep, sleep,

lit-tle one, sleep.

© Hallmark Licensing, Inc.

Sleep, Sleep, Little One, Sleep

The soothing quality of this melody stems from the use of a pentatonic (five-note) scale, which is common to much Oriental music (as well as some American folk music). The words constitute a "catalog" song (see "All The Pretty Little Horses," as well as "Hush, Little Baby"). Japanese parents would feel free to add toys, extending the list indefinitely. It is even said that, in different provinces of Japan, different toys are used in the lyrics, depending on local preferences.

Sleep, Sleep, Little One, Sleep

Japanese

Slowly
Am

mp

With pedal

Sleep,   sleep,_____   lit - tle   one,_____
Do   you   re -   call   that   nan -   ny

lie   down   and   go   to _____   sleep.
left   on   a   trip   to -   day?

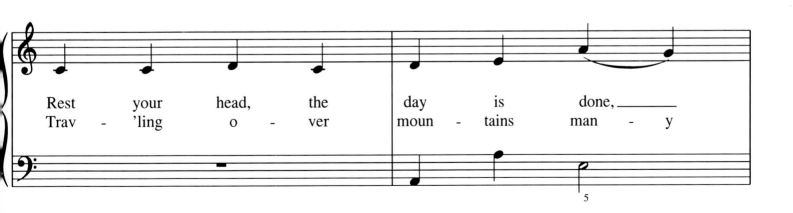

Rest   your   head,   the   day   is   done,_____
Trav - 'ling   o -   ver   moun - tains   man -   y

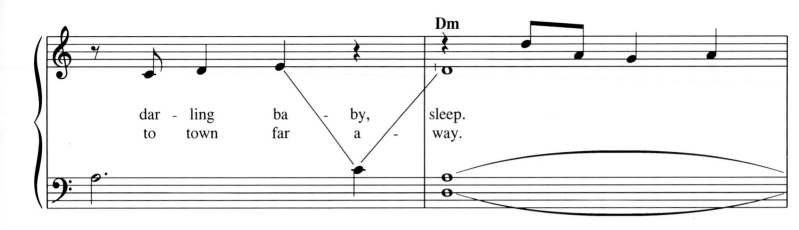

dar - ling ba - by, sleep.
to town far a - way.

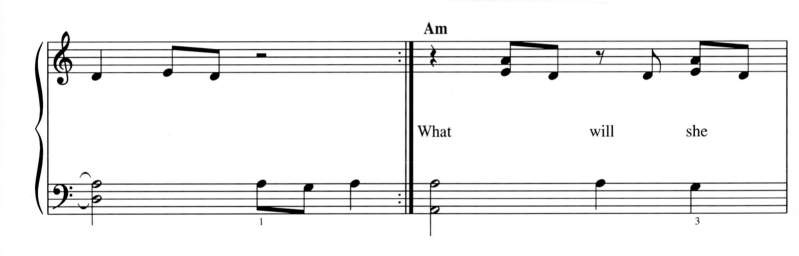

What will she

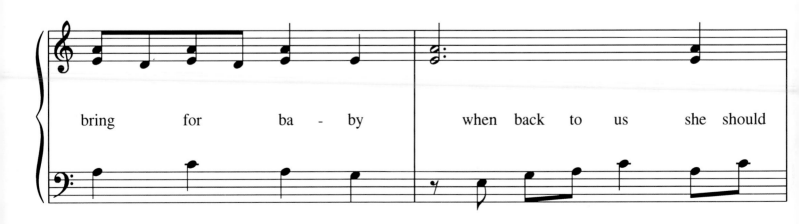

bring for ba - by when back to us she should

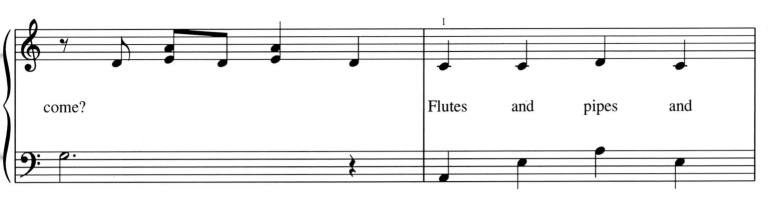

come?   Flutes   and   pipes   and

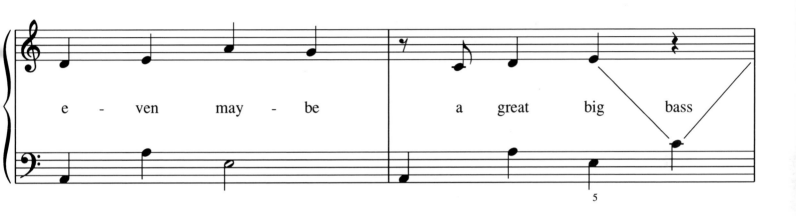

e - ven   may - be   a   great   big   bass

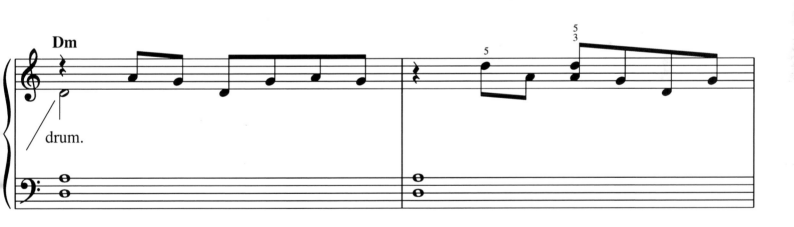

drum.

"WHAT IS IMPORTANT IS THAT
MY CHILDREN GROW UP
TO BE BEAUTIFUL IN THE HEART."
---Quote by Zumkit, Nyinban woman

Suliram
(Go To Sleep)

The sentiments of this lullaby are as powerful as they are simple: "Sleep well. I have waited for you so long; now that you're here, I'll hold onto you forever." These are thoughts that are echoed the world over, and they are accompanied here by a melody as simple and beautiful as the words.

Suliram
(Go To Sleep)

Indonesian

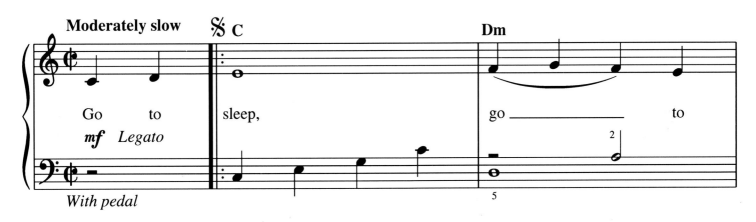

Go to sleep, go _____ to

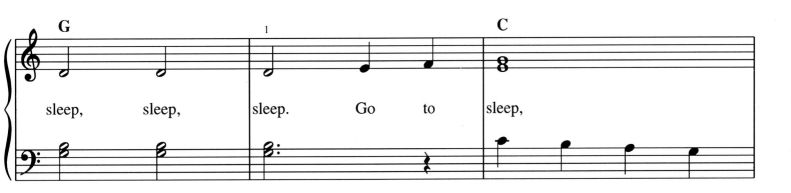

sleep, sleep, sleep. Go to sleep,

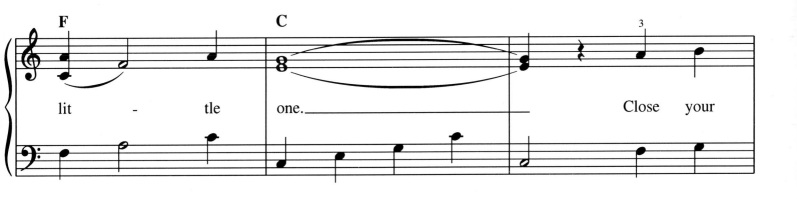

lit - tle one. _____ Close your

eyes and dream ___ ten - der dreams, ___

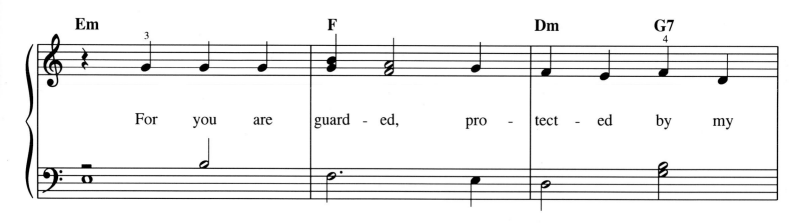

For you are guard - ed, pro - tect - ed by my

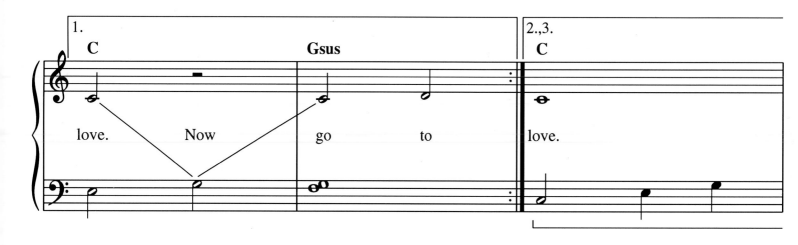

1.
love. Now go to

2.,3.
love.

Fine Slower
Long have I wait - ed, I've

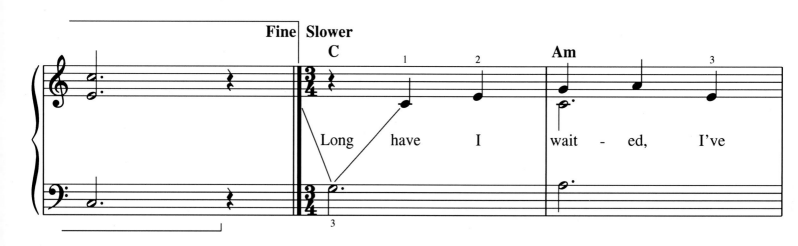

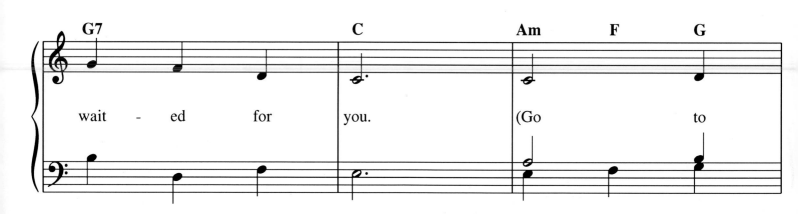

wait - ed for you. (Go to

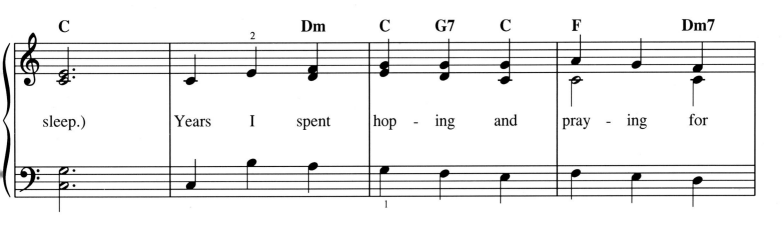

C   **Dm**   **C**   **G7**   **C**   **F**   **Dm7**

sleep.)   Years   I   spent   hop - ing   and   pray - ing   for

Tempo I

C   **Am**   **G7sus**   **C**

you.   (Go   to   sleep.)   Now   that   I

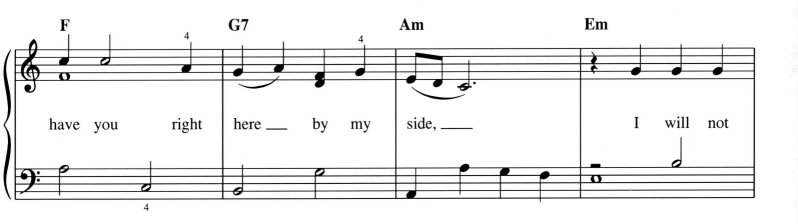

F   **G7**   **Am**   **Em**

have   you   right   here __ by   my   side, ____   I   will   not

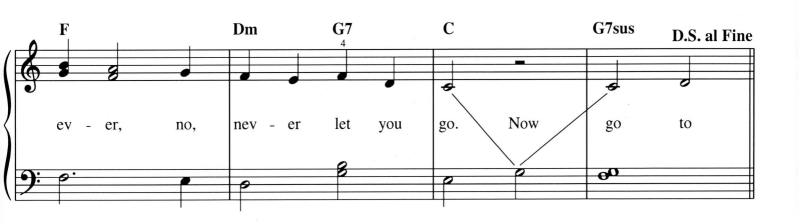

F   **Dm**   **G7**   **C**   **G7sus**   **D.S. al Fine**

ev - er,   no,   nev - er   let   you   go.   Now   go   to

Sweet And Low

Here we encounter a familiar picture: the mother assuring her child that father, who is away, will come back soon. (See also "Bye Baby Bunting," "Can Ye Sew Cushions," and "Sleep, Baby, Sleep.") But this is not a folk song. The words were written by Alfred Lord Tennyson (1809–1892) in 1850, about the time he was named Poet Laureate of England. Sir Joseph Barnby (1838–1896), composer and choral conductor, wrote the music 13 years later.

Sweet And Low

British

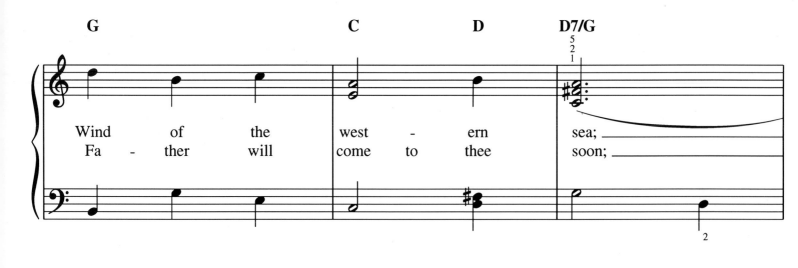

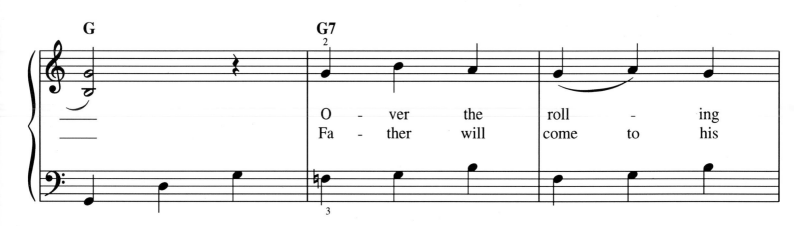

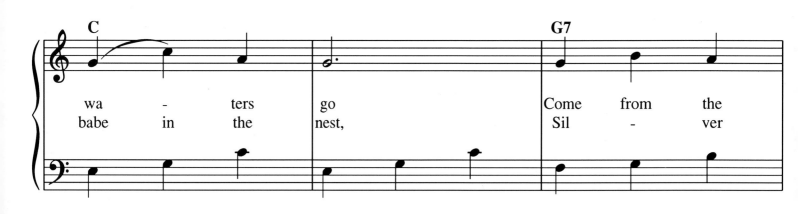

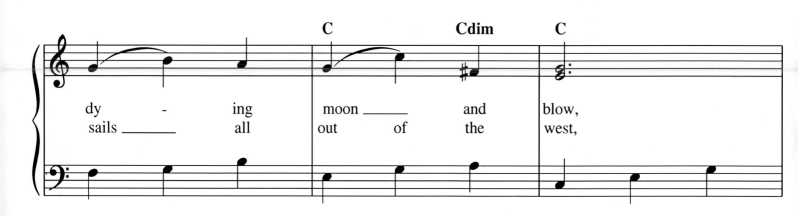

© Hallmark Licensing, Inc.

Too-Ra-Loo-Ra-Loo-Ral
(That's An Irish Lullaby)

Though thoroughly Irish in spirit, this song does not actually come from Ireland. James R. Shannon, who wrote the words and music, was a native-born American, albeit of Irish descent. This song was published in New York in 1913; it was one of many written during that era to appeal to the legion of Irish immigrants and their offspring who longed for a taste of the Emerald Isle.

Too-Ra-Loo-Ra-Loo-Ral
(That's An Irish Lullaby)

Irish

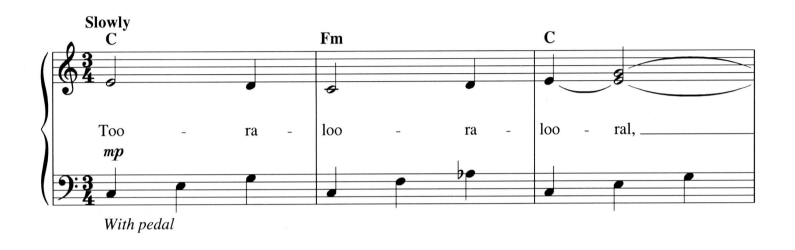

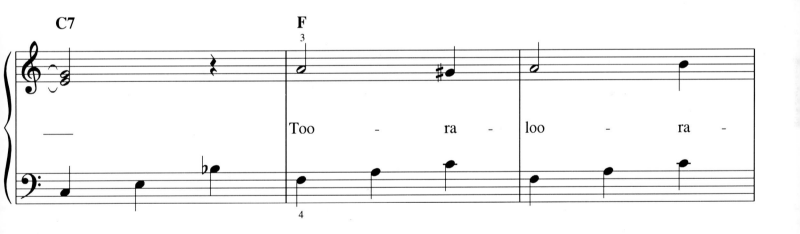

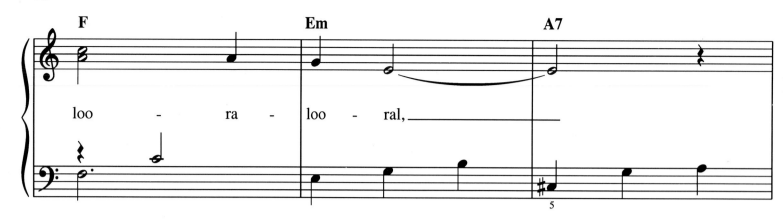

loo - ra - loo - ral,_____

Hush, now, don't you cry!_____

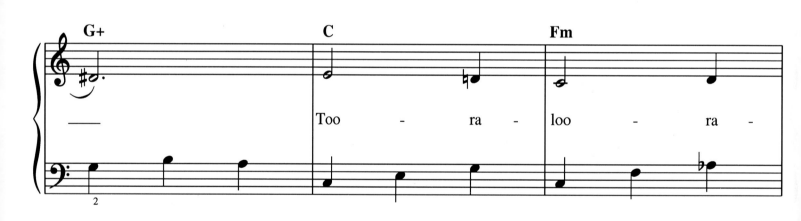

_____ Too - ra - loo - ra -

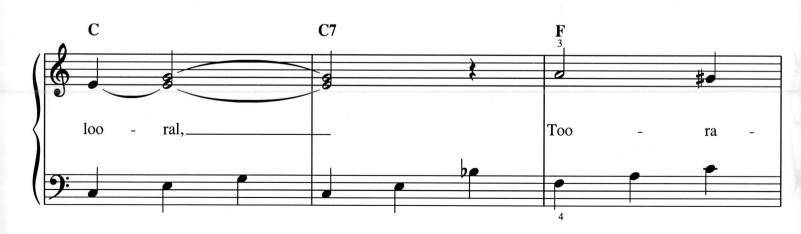

loo - ral,_____ Too - ra -

Twinkle, Twinkle, Little Star

The French tune "Ah! Vous Dirai-je, Maman" was first printed in 1761. It subsequently was given new words in England ("Baa, Baa, Black Sheep"), Germany ("Ist Das Nicht Ein Schnitzelbank"), and the United States ("A B C D E F G")—as well as being used by Mozart as the theme for a set of variations for piano. Meanwhile, British author Jane Taylor published a children's poem titled "The Star" in 1806. In 1881 a songbook published in the United States joined those words with the afore-mentioned music for the first time. French tune, British words, assembled in America. It seems some lullabies go around the world before they're ever sung!

American

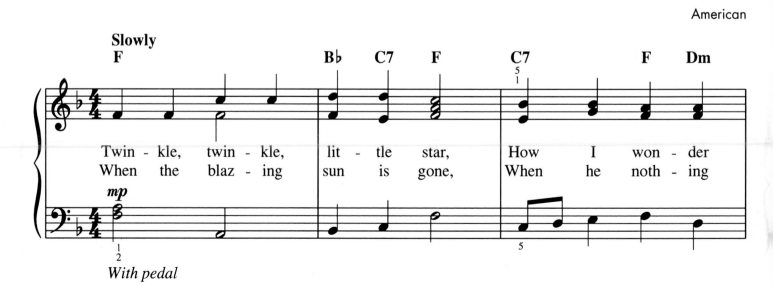